And
to
Every
Beast . . .

Treasures of the Vatican Library
(Book Illustration)

And
to
Every
Beast . . .

Turner Publishing, Inc.

ATLANTA

The illustrations in this book are taken from Latin volume 276
in the Urbino Collection, The Vatican Library.

Published by Turner Publishing, Inc.
A Subsidiary of Turner Broadcasting System, Inc.
1050 Techwood Drive, N.W.
Atlanta, Georgia 30318

First Edition 10 9 8 7 6 5 4 3 2 1
ISBN: 1-57036-101-0

Printed in the U.S.A.

Treasures of the Vatican Library:
Book Illustration

$\mathcal{A}$ND TO EVERY BEAST . . ., a small volume in the Treasures of the
Vatican Library series, offers a selection of miniature masterworks of book
illustration from the collections of one of the world's greatest repositories of
classical, medieval, and Renaissance culture. The Vatican Library, for six
hundred years celebrated as a center of learning and a monument to the art
of the book, is, nevertheless, little known to the general public, for
admission to the library traditionally has been restricted to qualified
scholars. Since very few outside the scholarly community have ever been
privileged to examine the magnificent hand-lettered and illuminated
manuscript books in the library's collections, the artwork selected for the
series volumes is all the more poignant, fascinating, and appealing.

Of course, the popes had always maintained a library, but in the fifteenth
century, Pope Nicholas V decided to build an edifice of unrivaled mag-
nificence to house the papacy's growing collections—to serve the entire
"court of Rome," the clerics and scholars associated with the papal palace.
Pope Sixtus IV added to what Nicholas had begun, providing the library with
a suite of beautifully frescoed rooms and furnishing it with heavy wooden

benches, to which the precious works were actually chained. But, most significantly, like the popes who succeeded him, Sixtus added books. By 1455 the library held 1,200 volumes, and a catalogue compiled in 1481 listed 3,500, making it by far the largest collection of books in the Western world.

And the Vatican Library has kept growing: through purchase, commission, donation, and military conquest. Nor did the popes restrict themselves to ecclesiastical subjects. Bibles, theological texts, and commentaries on canon law are here in abundance, to be sure, but so are the Latin and Greek classics that placed the Vatican Library at the very heart of all Renaissance learning. Over the centuries, the library has acquired some of world's most significant collections of literary works, including the Palatine Library of Heidelberg, the Cerulli collection of Persian and Ethiopian manuscripts, the great Renaissance libraries of the Duke of Urbino and of Queen Christiana of Sweden, and the matchless seventeenth-century collections of the Barberini, the Ottoboni, and Chigi. Today the library contains over one million printed books—including eight thousand published during the first fifty years of the printing press—in addition to 150,000 manuscripts and some 100,000 prints. Assiduously collected and carefully preserved over the course of almost six hundred years, these unique works of art and knowledge, ranging from the secular to the profane, are featured in this ongoing series, Treasures of the Vatican Library, for the delectation of lovers of great books and breathtaking works of art.

"And to every beast of the earth,
and to every bird of the air,
and to everything that creeps
on the earth, everything that has
the breath of life, I have given
every green plant for food."
And it was so.

GENESIS 1:30

. . . every wild animal of every kind, and all domestic animals of every kind, and every creeping thing that creeps on the earth, and every bird of every kind— every bird, every winged creature. They went into the ark with Noah, two and two of all flesh in which there was the breath of life.

GENESIS 7:14–15

Every creature loves its like, and
every person the neighbor. All
living beings associate with their
own kind, and
people stick close
to those like
themselves. What
does a wolf have in
common with a lamb?

ECCLESIASTICUS 13:15–17

So out of the ground the Lord God
formed every animal of the field
and every bird of the air, and
brought them to the man to see

what he would call them; and

whatever the man called every

living creature, that was its name.

Then the Lord God said to the woman, "What is this that you have done?" The woman said, "The serpent tricked me, and I ate."

The Lord God said to the serpent,
"Because you have done this, cursed
are you among all animals and
among all wild creatures; upon your
belly you shall go, and dust you
shall eat all the days of your life."

GENESIS 3:13–14

But the Lord provided a large fish to swallow up Jonah; and Jonah was in the belly of the fish three days and three nights.

JONAH 1:17

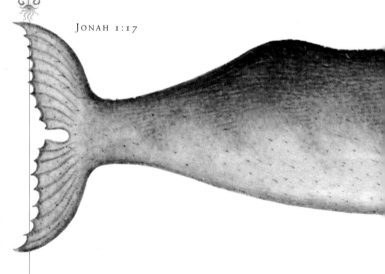

The voice of my beloved! Look, he comes, leaping upon the mountains, bounding over the hills. My beloved is like a gazelle or a young stag. Look, there he stands behind our wall, gazing in at the windows, looking through the lattice.

SONG OF SOLOMON 2:8–9

. . . when a bird flies through the air, no evidence of its passage is found; the light air, lashed by the beat of its pinions and pierced by the force of its rushing flight, is traversed by the movement of its wings, and afterward no sign of its coming is found there . . .

THE WISDOM OF SOLOMON 5:11

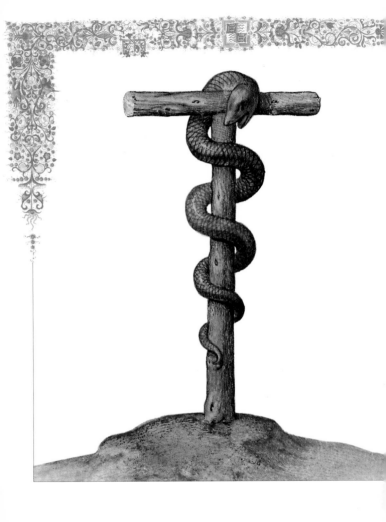

Who pities a snake charmer when he is bitten, or all those who go near wild animals? So no one pities a person who associates with a sinner and becomes involved in the other's sins.

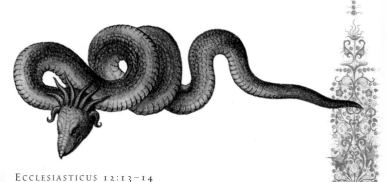

ECCLESIASTICUS 12:13–14

Does a lion roar in the forest, when it has no prey? Does a young lion cry out from its den, if it has caught nothing? Does a bird fall into a snare on the earth, when there is no trap for it? Does a snare spring up from the ground, when it has taken nothing?

Amos 3:4–5

. . . *the lizard can be grasped*

in the hand, yet it is found in

kings' palaces.

PROVERBS 30:28

He was driven from
human society, and his mind
was made like that of an animal.
His dwelling was with the wild
asses, he was fed grass like oxen,
and his body was bathed with the
dew of heaven. . . .

DANIEL 5:21

I am like an owl of the

wilderness, like a little owl of

the waste places. I lie awake;

I am like a lonely bird

on the housetop.

PSALMS 102:6–7

For every species of beast and bird, of reptile and sea creature, can be tamed and has been tamed by the human species, but no one can tame the tongue—a restless evil, full of deadly poison.

JAMES 3:7–8

Let the human race lament, but let
the wild animals of the field be
glad; let all who have been born
lament, but let the cattle and the
flocks rejoice. It is much better with
them than with us; for they do not
look for a judgment, and they do not
know of any torment or salvation
promised to them after death.

2 ESDRAS 7:65–66

Feasts are made for laughter; wine gladdens life, and money meets every need. Do not curse the king, even in your thoughts, or curse the rich, even in your bedroom; for a bird of the air may carry your voice, or some winged creature tell the matter.

ECCLESIASTES 10:19–20

Deliver my soul from the sword,

my life from the power of the dog!

Save me from the mouth of the

lion! From the horns of the wild

oxen you have rescued me.

But a stupid person will get understanding, when a wild ass is born human.

JOB 11:12

The beast that you saw was, and is not, and is about to ascend from the bottomless pit and go to destruction. And the inhabitants of the earth, whose names have not been written in the book of life from the foundation of the world, will be amazed when they see the beast, because it was and is not and is to come.

REVELATIONS 17:8

What peace is there between a hyena and a dog? And what peace between the rich and the poor?

ECCLESIASTICUS 13:18

A firstborn bull—majesty is his!
His horns are the horns of a wild
ox; with them he gores the
peoples, driving them to the ends
of the earth; . . .

DEUTERONOMY 33:17

I looked up and saw a ram standing beside the river. It had two horns. Both horns were long, but one was longer than the other, and the longer one came up second. I saw the ram charging westward and northward and southward. All beasts were powerless to withstand it, and no one could rescue from its power; it did as it pleased and became strong.

DANIEL 8:3–4

Do not deliver the soul of your dove to the wild animals; do not forget the life of your poor forever.

PSALMS 74:19

And the beast that I saw was like
a leopard, its feet were like a
bear's, and its mouth was like
a lion's mouth. . . .

REVELATIONS 13:2

My heart is in anguish within me,
the terrors of death have fallen
upon me. Fear and trembling come
upon me, and horror overwhelms
me. And I say, "O that I had
wings like a dove! I would fly
away and be
at rest . . ."

PSALMS 55:4–6

. . .Through a land of trouble and
distress, of lioness and roaring
lion, of viper and flying serpent,
they carry their riches
on the backs of donkeys. . . .

ISAIAH 30:6

When my soul was
embittered, when I was
pricked in heart,

I was stupid and ignorant;

I was like a brute beast

toward you.

PSALMS 73:21-22

". . . There is no rest day or night for those who worship the beast and its image and for anyone who receives the mark of its name."

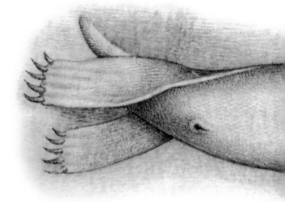

REVELATIONS 14:11

The trees of the Lord are watered abundantly, the cedars of Lebanon that he planted. In them the birds build their nests; the stork has its home in the fir trees. The high mountains are for the wild goats; the rocks are a refuge for the coneys.

PSALMS 104:16–18

I will make for you a covenant on
that day with the wild animals,
the birds of the air, and the
creeping things of the ground; and

*I will abolish the bow, the sword,
and war from the land; and I will
make you lie down in safety.*

HOSEA 2:18

Three things are stately in their stride; four are stately in their gait: the lion, which is mightiest among wild animals and does not turn back before any; the strutting rooster, the he-goat, and a king striding before his people.

PROVERBS 30:29-31

I adjure you, O daughters of Jerusalem, by the gazelles or the wild does: do not stir up or awaken love until it is ready!

SONG OF SOLOMON 2:7

The great dragon was thrown
down, that ancient serpent,
who is called the Devil and
Satan, the deceiver of the whole
world—he was thrown down to
the earth, and his angels were
thrown down with him.

REVELATIONS 12:9

. . . and four
great beasts came
up out of the sea,
different from one another.
The first was like a lion and had
eagles' wings. Then, as I watched,
its wings were plucked off, and it
as lifted up from the ground and
made to stand on two feet
like a human being; . . .

DANIEL 7:3-4

And I saw three foul spirits like frogs coming from the mouth of the dragon, from the mouth of the beast, and from the mouth of the false prophet.

Revelations 16:13

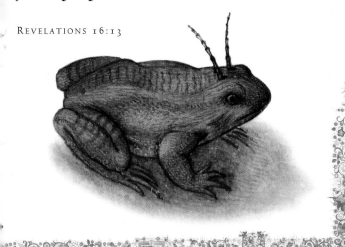

. . . the locusts have no king,

yet all of them march in rank; . . .

PROVERBS 30:27

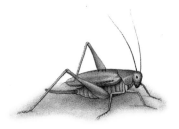